Cherish your dreams, hold tight to your ideals, march boldly to the music that only you can hear. Great lives are built by moving forward, never by looking back.

Even in our darkest moments, Americans have always had hope. By remembering our history, holding on to our values, and supporting each other, we have found the strength to face any struggle thrown our way.

GOD BLESS THE U.S.A.

LEE GREENWOOD

Rutledge Hill Press®
A Division of Thomas Nelson, Inc.

Nashville, Tennessee
www.ThomasNelson.com

Published by Rutledge Hill Press, a Division of Thomas Nelson, Inc., P.O. Box 141000, Nashville, Tennessee 37214. www.ThomasNelson.com

Design: Lookout Design Group, Inc., Minneapolis, MN

ISBN: 1-55853-987-5

Printed in the United States of America

01 02 03 04 05—5 4 3 2 1

Your purchase of *God Bless the U.S.A.* will benefit

Since 1982, AmeriCares has delivered nearly $3 billion worth of humanitarian assistance to 137 nations, providing emergency response as well as supporting long-term healthcare programs around the world. It has a worldwide system of distribution centers, including a twenty-four-hour disaster warehouse in Connecticut that provides immediate response to emergencies around the globe. In the United States, AmeriCares operates three free clinics, a home repair project that aids the poor and elderly, and a summer camp for children with HIV/AIDS and other life-threatening illnesses. AmeriCares has a remarkably low overhead, consistently under 2 percent, but more importantly, the individuals who are part of AmeriCares share a mission of providing help and hope— immediately and efficiently—to victims around the world.

AmeriCares
161 Cherry Street
New Canaan, CT 06840
1–800–486–HELP (4357)

I'm sometimes overwhelmed by this vast nation and wish I could see how America will change in the next one hundred years. As long as we continue to dream, create inventions, and solve the challenges of an ever-expanding population, we will have the power to create a better society. But it is inevitable that the freedom, liberty, and can-do attitude that characterize us will be challenged, sometimes in ways that leave us no choice but to defend ourselves and the land we love. It happened in 1941 at Pearl Harbor and again in 2001 at the World Trade Center and the Pentagon.

I wrote "God Bless the U.S.A." in 1983 to bring people together. We have our differences and that is one of the many strengths of our country. But even if we don't agree on economics or politics, I hope this song can let us sing together as Americans and perhaps our differences won't matter so much.

I pray that God, who has watched over this nation for more than two hundred years, will not forsake us. And I pray that God would keep us safe from those who would do us harm. I pray for America, "'cause there ain't no doubt I love this land. God Bless the U.S.A."

Lee Greenwood

Lee Greenwood

GOD BLESS THE U.S.A.

If tomorrow all the things were gone
I'd worked for all my life,
And I had to start again
with just my children and my wife,
I'd thank my lucky stars
to be living here today,
'Cause the flag still stands for freedom
and they can't take that away.

I'm proud to be an American
where at least I know I'm free,
And I won't forget the men who died
who gave that right to me,
And I gladly stand up next to you
and defend her still today,
'Cause there ain't no doubt I love this land
GOD BLESS THE U.S.A.

From the lakes of Minnesota
to the hills of Tennessee
Across the plains of Texas
from sea to shining sea.
From Detroit down to Houston
and New York to L.A.,
There's pride in every American heart
and it's time we stand and say:

I'm proud to be an American
where at least I know I'm free,
And I won't forget the men who died
who gave that right to me,
And I gladly stand up next to you
and defend her still today,
'Cause there ain't no doubt I love this land
GOD BLESS THE U.S.A.

★ ★ ★

"Let every nation know, whether it wishes us well or ill, we shall pay any price, bear any burden, meet any hardship, support any friend, oppose any foe, TO ASSURE THE SURVIVAL AND SUCCESS OF LIBERTY."

—*John F. Kennedy*

Five Marines and a Navy corpsman raise the American flag on top of a mountain on Iwo Jima at the end of World War II.

"We are not weak if we make proper use of those means which the God of nature hath placed in our power. . . . The battle, sir, is not to the strong alone; it is to the vigilant, the active, the brave." — PATRICK HENRY

I pledge allegiance to the flag

of the United States of America

and to the Republic for which it stands,

ONE NATION UNDER GOD,

INDIVISIBLE,

with liberty and justice for all.

IF TOMORROW ALL THE THINGS WERE GONE

I'D WORKED FOR ALL MY LIFE,

AND I HAD TO START AGAIN

WITH JUST MY CHILDREN AND MY WIFE,

"*All* is not lost. Though four hundred million dollars worth of property has been destroyed, Chicago still exists. The lake, the spacious harbor, the vast empire of production, the great arteries of trade and commerce all remain. We have lost money, but we have saved life, health, vigor, and industry."

—*Joseph Medill,* EDITORIAL IN THE *Chicago Tribune,* OCTOBER 1871, AFTER THE GREAT CHICAGO FIRE DESTROYED 73,000 MILES OF STREETS AND 17,500 BUILDINGS AND LEFT 100,000 PERSONS HOMELESS

Few cities have been destroyed as completely as was the heart of Chicago in 1871

I'D THANK MY LUCKY

TO BE LIVING HERE TODAY,

'CAUSE THE FLAG STILL

AND THEY CAN'T

STARS

STANDS FOR FREEDOM

TAKE THAT AWAY

"Yesterday, the greatest question was decided which ever was debated in America; and a greater perhaps never was, nor will be, decided among men. A resolution was passed without one dissenting colony, that those United Colonies are, and of right ought to be, free and independent States."

— *John Adams* (LETTER TO MRS. ADAMS, JULY 3, 1776)

I'M PROUD TO

WHERE AT LEAST

AND I WON'T FORGET

THE MEN WHO DIED

WHO GAVE THAT RIGHT TO ME,

BE AN AMERICAN

KNOW I'M FREE,

THOMAS J KORDO

DENNIS W SMITH · ROBERT G RO

VINCIGUERRA · VERNON M WIG

PATRICK H HALBERT · RICHARD J HA

RAYMOND PLATERO · ROBERT W R

WILLIAM L WOOD · ERICK W

PRESTON L HALL · EVE

Stop for just a minute.

Take an inventory of all the things in your life you have to be thankful for.

Have you told those responsible how much you appreciate them?

WRITE LETTERS.

MAKE CALLS.

TELL THEM IN PERSON.

Tell your teachers, your leaders, your police officers, your family, your friends, your employer.

Tell them, "Thank you."

"Double—no triple—our troubles and we'd still be better off than any other people on earth."—RONALD REAGAN

AND I GLADLY STAND UP

AND DEFEND HER STILL TODAY,

'CAUSE THERE AIN'T NO

GOD BLESS

NEXT TO YOU

DOUBT I LOVE THIS LAND

THE U.S.A.

"Freedom

—no word was ever spoken that has held out greater hope, demanded greater sacrifice, needed to be nurtured, blessed more the giver, damned more its destroyer, or come closer to being God's will on earth. AND I THINK THAT'S WORTH FIGHTING FOR, IF NECESSARY."

—*General Omar N. Bradley*

"And so, my fellow Americans, ask not what your country can do for you; ask what you can do for your country." —JOHN F. KENNEDY

"Some people give time, some give money, some their skills and connections, some literally give their life's blood. But everyone has something to give." — *Barbara Bush*

"In the future days which we seek to make secure, we look forward to a world founded upon four essential human freedoms.

THE FIRST IS freedom of speech and expression—everywhere in the world.

THE SECOND IS freedom of every person to worship God in his own way—everywhere in the world.

THE THIRD IS freedom from want . . . —everywhere in the world.

THE FOURTH IS freedom from fear . . . —anywhere in the world. . . .

The world order which we seek is the cooperation of free countries, working together in a friendly, civilized society. This nation has placed its destiny in the hands, heads and hearts of its millions of free men and women, and its faith in freedom under the guidance of God. Freedom means the supremacy of human rights everywhere. Our support goes to those who struggle to gain those rights and keep them. Our strength is our unity of purpose. To that high concept, there can be no end save victory."

— *Franklin Delano Roosevelt,*

JANUARY 6, 1941

I have a dream that one day this nation will rise up and live out the true meaning of its creed: 'We hold these truths to be self-evident that all men are created equal.' . . . I have a dream that my four little children will one day live in a nation where they will not be judged by the color of their skin but by their character. . . . With this faith we will be able to transform the jangling discords of our nation into a beautiful symphony of brotherhood. . . . And if America is to be a great nation, this must become true. So let freedom ring from the hilltops of New Hampshire. Let freedom ring from the mighty mountains of New York. Let freedom ring from the heightening Alleghenies of Pennsylvania.

Let freedom ring from the snow-capped Rockies of Colorado. Let freedom ring from the curvaceous slopes of California. But not only that, let freedom ring from Stone Mountain of Georgia. Let freedom ring from every hill and molehill of Mississippi and every mountainside. When we let freedom ring, when we let it ring from every tenement and every hamlet, from every state and every city, we will be able to speed up that day when all of God's children, black men and white men, Jews and Gentiles, Protestants and Catholics, will be able to join hands and sing in the words of the old spiritual, 'Free at last, free at last, Thank God Almighty, we are free at last.' "

—MARTIN LUTHER KING, JR., *August 28, 1963*

There's a brand new wind a-blowin' down that Lincoln road.

There's a brand new hope a-growin' down where freedom's seeds are sowed.

There's a new truth we'll be knowin' that will lift our heavy load,

When we find out what free men can really do.

There's a brand new day a-comin' for the land called U.S.A.

New tunes we'll be a-strummin' in our hearts by night and day.

As we march on we'll be hummin', how our troubles' gone away,

'Cause we've found out what free men can really do.

And if you feel like dancin' then, why come on folks, and dance!

And if you feel like prancin' then, why come on folks, and prance!

'Cause I really ain't romancin' when I say we've got our chance

To show 'em what free men can really do.

There's a brand new wind a-blowin' thru a land that's proud and free.

Ev'rywhere there's folks a-wakin' to a truth that's bound to be.

So let's all pull together for that day of victory,

And we'll show 'em what free men can really do!

— LANGSTON HUGHES

★ ★ ★

"America has continued to rise through every age against every challenge, a people of great works and greater possibilities, who have always, always found the wisdom and strength to come together as one nation, to widen the circle of opportunity, to deepen the meaning of freedom to form that more perfect union."

— BILL CLINTON

"What constitutes an American? Not color nor race nor religion. Not the pedigree of his family nor the place of his birth. Not the coincidence of his citizenship. Not his social status nor his bank account. Not his trade nor his profession. An American is one who loves justice and believes in the dignity of man. An American is one who will fight for his freedom and that of his neighbor. An American is one who will sacrifice property, ease, and security in order that he and his children may retain the rights of free men. An American is one in whose heart is engraved the immortal second sentence of the Declaration of Independence.*"

— *Harold Ickes*, MAY 18, 1941

We hold these truths to be self-evident, that all men are created equal, that they are endowed by their Creator with certain unalienable Rights, that among these are Life, Liberty, and the pursuit of Happiness.

"A nation is formed by the willingness of each of us to share in the responsibility for upholding the common good." — *Barbara Jordan*

"*America did not invent human rights. In a very real sense . . .*

human rights invented America." — J I M M Y   C A R T E R

FROM THE LAKES OF MINNESOTA

TO THE HILLS OF TENNESSEE,

ACROSS THE

FROM SEA TO

PLAINS OF TEXAS

SHINING SEA.

★ ★ ★

"We must build a new world, a far better world—one in which the eternal dignity of man is respected." — HARRY S TRUMAN

"You can gain strength, courage and confidence by every experience in which you really stop to look fear in the face. . . . You must do the thing which you think you cannot do." — ELEANOR ROOSEVELT

THERE'S PRIDE IN

AND IT'S TIME WE

FROM DETROIT DOWN TO HOUSTON

AND NEW YORK TO L.A.,

EVERY AMERICAN HEART

STAND AND SAY:

"We here highly resolve that these dead shall not have died in vain, that this nation under God shall have a new birth of freedom, and that government of the people, by the people, for the people shall not perish from the earth."

— *Abraham Lincoln* (GETTYSBURG ADDRESS)

"Courage is the price life exacts for granting peace."

— AMELIA EARHART

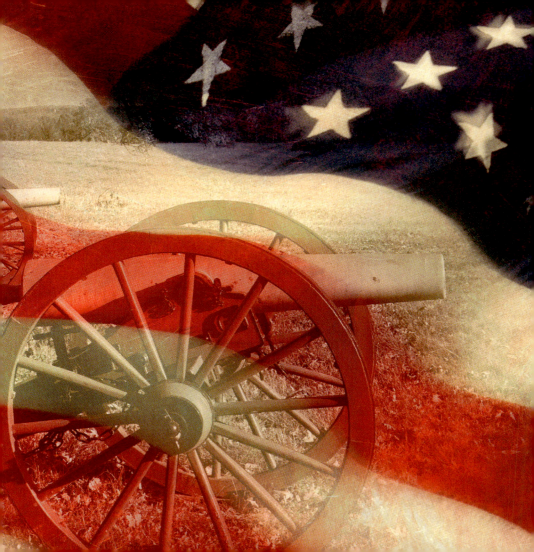

I'M PROUD TO BE AN AMERICAN

WHERE AT LEAST I KNOW I'M FREE

AND I WON'T FORGET THE MEN WHO DIED

WHO GAVE THAT RIGHT TO ME,

America is a land filled with courageous, giving people.

People who fight for what is right.

People who don't tolerate bullies.

People who are there in times of crisis.

And people who lend a hand.

BE PROUD TO CALL YOURSELF AN AMERICAN.

Help make this world, not just this country, a better place.

There is not anyone too old or too young,

too rich or too poor, to make a difference.

AND I GLADLY STAND UP NEXT TO YOU

AND DEFEND HER STILL TODAY,

'CAUSE THERE AIN'T NO DOUBT I LOVE THIS LAND

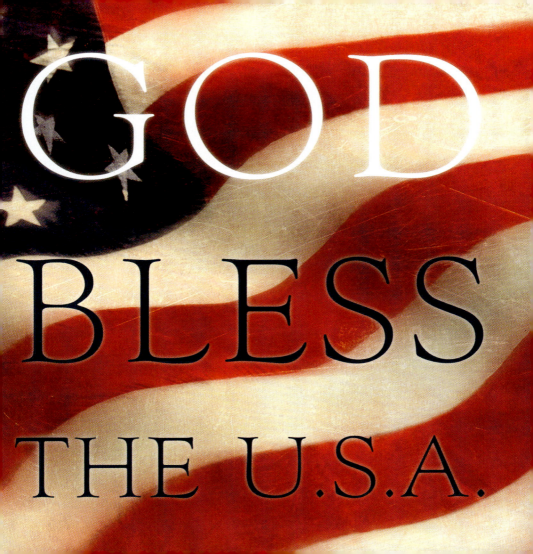

"We are going to have peace,
even if we have to fight for it."

— *Dwight Eisenhower*

"Tyranny, like hell, is not easily conquered; yet we have
this consolation with us, that
the harder the conflict, the
more glorious the triumph."

— THOMAS PAINE

"The tree of liberty must be refreshed from time to time with the blood of patriots and tyrants."

— THOMAS JEFFERSON

"With malice toward none, with charity for all, . . . let us finish the work we are in, to bind up the nation's wounds."

— ABRAHAM LINCOLN

"God, who gave us life, gave us liberty. Can the liberties of a nation be secure when we have removed a conviction that these liberties are the gift of God? Indeed, I tremble for my country when I reflect that God is just, that his justice cannot sleep forever." —THOMAS JEFFERSON

"If my people, which are called by my name, shall humble themselves, and pray, and seek my face, and turn from their wicked ways; then will I hear from heaven, and will forgive their sin, and will heal their land." (I CHRONICLES 7:14)

"We have a choice whether to implode and disintegrate emotionally and spiritually as a people and a nation, or whether we choose to become stronger through all of the struggle to rebuild on a solid foundation."

— *George W. Bush* AT A MEMORIAL SERVICE AT THE NATIONAL CATHEDRAL HONORING THOSE WHO LOST THEIR LIVES IN THE THE TERRORIST ATTACKS AT THE WORLD TRADE CENTER AND AT THE PENTAGON ON SEPTEMBER 11, 2001

Darkness CEASES *to exist*

when the light of ONE *flame still burns.*

"ONE MAN WITH COURAGE MAKES A MAJORITY."

—Andrew Jackson